Dream Big and Live Your Dreams

Geary Reid

ISBN: 978-976-8305-86-2.

Acknowledgments

Great thanks must be expressed to the following people:

The heavenly Father, for granting me the wisdom and inspiration to record the information in this book, which I began on March 3, 2022, and completed on March 6, 2022; my family, for their continued encouragement and support regarding various challenges; and several people who have assisted with reviewing and editing the book:

- Wonnetta Nicholson, Dipl. in Business Management and Administration
- Judah Louisy, MSc, ACCA, FCPA

To you, the reader: have fun while reading, and grasp and practice what you learn so that this world will become a better place. Many people are depending on your guidance. We all need a shoulder to lean on and a hand to guide us.

Geary Reid

MBA, FCCA, FAAPM, MPM, CAT

Reid's Learning Institute and Business Consultancy

reidnlearn.com

Amazon: amazon.com/author/gearyreid

Facebook: Reid n Learn

Instagram: Reid n Learn

LinkedIn: Reid's Learning Institute
and Business Consultancy

199 Kuru - Kururu, Soesdyke Linden Highway
Guyana, South America

Table of Contents

Introduction

Having big dreams is not a bad thing. Many persons do not know where they want to go, what they want to become, or what impact they plan to make. Those who do not yet know their dreams must start dreaming now. They must set their minds on big things that they want to see happen through them. Some persons need to move away from dreaming small to dreaming about great things.

Big dreams can make some persons fearful. They question whether they have the ability to bring those dreams to life. When there is fear, the mind does not function effectively. However, if people can overcome their fears and be confident that great things can happen through them, then they will begin to challenge themselves to fulfill their dreams.

Persons who have big dreams must avoid certain kinds of people. This includes toxic people who will try to do everything possible to discourage others from accomplishing their dreams. Oftentimes, toxic people do not want anyone to become better than they are. People with big dreams must avoid negative thinking and stop doubting themselves.

There must be a paradigm shift in the minds of those with self-doubt. If the mind is not prepared for success, then the body will act in defeat and denial.

Persons must make efforts to write down what they want to accomplish. When they fail to write down their dreams, they tend to forget about them. Writing them down allows the dreams to be fresh in their minds, and it also acts as a reference point when they are discouraged.

Everyone who wants to see their dream becoming reality must be prepared to work hard and smart. They cannot expect others to fulfill their dream for them while they are relaxing.

Learning to be quiet is something that many people must do when they have dreams. They cannot tell their dreams to everyone. They must also pray about their dreams so that they will receive guidance from the Creator.

Dreamers must also look for similar exposure, since they can learn many things that will make them successful. Persons with big dreams may experience failure, but they must push towards making their dreams come through. To overcome certain challenges, persons may need to align themselves with mentors.

Great planning will be necessary to make big dreams come through, so time must be allocated to various activities for each dream. After planning, dreamers must be willing to work hard at executing their plans. They must review past performance and see what they could do better if a similar situation occurs again. Persons must learn to celebrate their successes, both big and small, as they accomplish their dreams.

1. Having a dream

Having a big dream does not mean that someone has to sleep and then wake up with great ideas and inspiration. Persons can dream with their eyes wide open. Dreaming does not have to occur at night, but can happen at any time during the day. Everyone needs to have their own dream. For those who have not yet dreamed, they need to start dreaming.

When a person has a dream, it challenges them to change many aspects of their current situation to confirm the direction in which they will soon have to go. Because of their dreams, some persons do not settle for mediocrity. They are often challenged to keep going after their dreams.

1.1 What would you like to do?

A big question for future dreamers: what would you like to do? When people know what they want to do, then they will have the courage to live up to their dreams. However, if a person does not know what they would like to do, they will be comfortable doing the same old things for years.

Every dream has a pull factor in the life of the dreamer, which is what makes the dreamer uncomfortable. While other persons are comfortable with their current state of affairs, those who have dreams often want to work towards accomplishing those dreams, and this can cause them to have restless days and nights. Everywhere they go, they are reminded of their dream.

Persons can change their clothes in order to look different. However, when people have dreams, then even if they change their clothes, they will still have the same desire to go accomplish their dreams. A person's dream is not extrinsic to them, but intrinsic. Therefore, their dream is always within them, and they cannot run away from themselves.

1.2 What would you like to accomplish?

A dream often challenges persons to take appropriate actions. It makes them uncomfortable in their old position and demands that they make some changes.

Some people do not know their dream. However, they must search within themselves and see what it is that they want to accomplish. They may find that they have a burning desire to accomplish something.

When a person has a dream, it often keeps them awake as it stirs them to take action to accomplish their dream.

1.3 How do you want people to perceive you?

Oftentimes, dreamers want to be perceived for doing something important or different and to have a great impact on the minds of others. Dreamers know that they may only have a short period to make a great impact on others, so they may be stirred to make that impact as soon as possible. They know that they do not have the luxury of time on their side. They may feel that if they do not yield to their dream, someone else will do the same thing they wanted to do. They want others to know them as the one who implemented or first started something important.

1.4 Where do you want to go?

When they have a dream, people have to decide where they want to go. While other persons may be relaxing, dreamers have places to go. Once they know where they want to go, then they must get there quickly.

Getting to their destinations is pivotal for them. The road may be long, but they are willing to accelerate their speed to get there.

2. Avoid toxic people

Not everyone will be happy for the success of others. Some people wish that others would never succeed, so their minds are often toxic to those who have big dreams.

When some people know that they have not accomplished certain things, they hate it when anyone else becomes a success. Certain dreams cannot be shared with such persons, since they are dream-killers.

2.1 Stealing dreams

Some toxic persons are good at stealing dreams. They listen to what others tell them and then quickly try to implement those persons' dreams. They may not have any shame in duplicating other people's dreams and operating as though it was their own dream.

They often give listening ears to other persons' dreams and seek much information so that they can learn about the smallest details of those dreams. After they receive all the details they want, they start trying to implement that person's dream.

2.2 Discouragers

Some persons only have negative views to share. As they listen to other people talking about their big dreams, they will listen but provide many reasons why such dreams cannot become reality. These are the types of discouraging statements they may make:

- This dream will require much money, and you do not have the money to make it a reality
- No member of your family has accomplished such a dream
- You are too young to accomplish such a dream

- You are too old to accomplish such a dream
- No one in your community or country has accomplished such a dream
- You do not have the academics and experience for such a big dream
- Your color and size will not allow you to succeed

These are only some of the negative statements that toxic people make. Even when you do not ask them for an opinion, they are willing to share their negative views. Sometimes before you can even approach them, they approach you and keep reminding you not to follow through with that dream.

Some discouragements come from persons' companions or other relatives. Sometimes, people do not tell their dreams to their family because many of their family members are discouragers.

2.3 Set boundaries

To avoid toxic people and their negative views, it will be important to set boundaries. You will have to decide how much information to share with certain people, as it is important not to give them any fuel to start a fire. Let them search for their own fuel, and by the time they find it, you will have accomplished your dreams.

It may be important to restrict the level of access some persons have in one's personal life. For those who once had toxic people visiting them frequently, they may need to restrict their future visits.

Try as hard as possible to keep toxic people away from important information and places.

2.4 Change friendships

Those who are passionate about going after their dreams may have to change their friendships. Some persons who were very close to them must not be given the same privilege they once had. These changes will be necessary to allow persons to fulfill their dreams.

It may hurt at the beginning to discontinue friendships with some people. However, this may be the best approach to avoid toxic people.

2.5 Stop sharing dreams and details with toxic people

Carefully decide what to share with certain persons, and stop sharing your dreams with those who are toxic. Keep them away from all sensitive information. It may hurt you to make such drastic changes, but you are only preserving yourself and your dream.

While they may recognize some differences in you, you do not have to explain to them why you have made these changes. You are not obligated to keep them informed of all details, so do not be apologetic to them.

If you know that a toxic person does not want you to be successful, then avoid them for the future, even if you were friends with them for many years. It is better that you avoid them and fulfill your dream, rather than maintain the friendship and kill your dream.

2.6 Avoid toxic people, but accept constructive criticism

A big challenge that some persons have is that they do not like to accept constructive criticism. While they have big dreams, they may be given good advice on what they must do to make their dreams become reality. Constructive criticism can come from young or old persons, from friends or family members, or from anyone else. Sometimes, these persons have had similar experiences and want to share their journey. Some of these individuals might have seen other persons struggle in the same area, so they are ready to share their important guidance.

However, when many people have big dreams, they often do not want anyone to give them some guidance. They may believe that everyone who speaks to them is a toxic person. Even the negative statements from one's enemies may be good learning opportunities and will help the listener to make great decisions.

Not everyone can accept constructive criticism and make the necessary adjustments to realize their dreams. When some persons receive advice from others that does not sound positive, they feel that those persons hate them. But that may be far from the truth. Some people love them and only want to tell them what they need to do to fulfill their big dreams.

3. Avoid negative thinking

Not everyone believes in themselves when they have big dreams. As a matter of fact, some people start to doubt themselves. They think about their background and all the negative things that have happened to them, and they second-guess themselves.

Those who have big dreams may tell their dreams to their friends, and if those friends respond negatively, it may cause them to doubt themselves. When people keep doubting themselves about their big dreams, they will not work towards fulfilling those dreams.

3.1 Avoid certain news reports

Many people will listen to the daily news or read newspapers. Radio, television, and newspapers will include good and bad news. Persons must be selective in terms of what they listen to or read. To avoid bad feelings and negative thinking, certain news reports must be avoided.

For example, the news may report about vehicular accidents, murder, divorce, domestic violence, poverty, economic hardship, etc. Reports about these news items may make the listener very sad, rather than happy.

3.2 Avoid listening to certain politicians

When it is close to an election, politicians often make many speeches, some of which never become reality. Some politicians will speak without giving much consideration to what they are saying. Their speeches are often intended to make their own political party sound better than all the others.

Oftentimes, politicians will try to pull down the image of another contender. They may say things that sound nice to the audience but are not truthful.

4. Paradigm shifts

Persons who have big dreams sometimes need a paradigm shift. They must stop thinking about small things and begin to think of big things. They must cease to think of defeat and think of success instead.

With this paradigm shift, they will have to allow themselves to see new possibilities. Oftentimes, big dreams will demand that people do great things. Big dreams will cause some people to shift out of their comfort zone. As their minds awaken to great things, they will have to challenge their bodies to come into alignment with their thinking, as the human body often works along with the mind. Therefore, if the mind does not have a revolution in thinking, the body will continue to do the same things.

4.1 Listen to positive people

When a person wants to move away from negative thinking, they can do so by listening to people who think and act positively. Such persons spend much time motivating others. Most of the words uttered from their mouths will uplift others, and they do not spend time pulling down other people.

Positive-thinking people will allow others to see their big dreams as something that is possible to accomplish. Positive-thinking people are not afraid to share thoughts with others about how they can become successful, because positive-thinking people are not intimidated by others.

4.2 Listen to successful people

When a person wants to be successful, they must learn to mix with others who are already successful. Those who are successful will often act as encouragers for those who do not think that they can accomplish their dreams.

Successful people will often share their good and bad stories. They may share about the number of times that they failed but did not give up, as well as some of the secrets that enabled them to become successful.

4.3 Listen to motivational songs

Listening to songs that motivate is another way for persons to change their mindset and find the courage to go after their dreams. Motivational songs will cause persons with big dreams to keep their eyes focused on their dreams, no matter how challenging their dreams appear to be.

When people have big dreams, they may doubt themselves. They may not have many people they can talk to about their dreams. However, as they listen to motivational songs, they will keep doing what is necessary for the success of their dreams.

4.4 Watch life-changing and motivational movies

Those who need to avoid negative thinking can watch movies that make them feel great. Horror movies will not work in their favor.

After watching certain movies, people feel upbeat and want to go after their dreams. Some movies have good messages that inspire those who watch them to do great things. After they watch those movies, they feel energized to do what once seemed impossible.

Some movies can change lives. For example, those who are struggling with anger may be inspired to change their behavior after they watch life-changing movies.

4.5 Go places that will uplift your spirit

In an effort to fulfill their dreams, some persons may have to go places where they can relax. When they visit such places, they will have new ideas or bursts of energy for accomplishing their dreams.

Visiting places like nature resorts, spending time by running water, visiting animals, attending religious services, and visiting other countries are some ways that persons can change in their thinking by going someplace uplifting.

Attending sporting events may make people energized to go after their dreams. Those whose team wins may return home feeling motivated and having positive thoughts about their own ability to be successful.

4.6 Participate in physical exercise

Some persons find that physical exercise helps them to remain positive. They may choose to exercise daily because it gives them the courage to utilize their energy and time for good purposes. Exercising will help to burn energy, and it may cause some persons to get rid of anger and anxiety. As persons exercise, they will remain focused. This means they will have to remain positive in order to avoid doing things that can result in physical injuries while exercising.

5. Equip yourself with the necessary resources

Everyone that has a dream must do certain things. No dream will become a reality unless people put time and effort into accomplishing their dreams. There are many persons who are waiting for their big dreams to independently unfold in their lives, but that will not happen, since they must do things to activate their dreams.

For example, a dream is like having a seed in a storage container. As long as the seed remains stored away, nothing will happen. If the person wants a great harvest from that seed, then they have to prepare the soil, ensure that the temporary moisture is acceptable to the seed, and then place the seed in the soil. After a certain number of days, the seed will germinate, and then the planter has to transplant the seed into the earth.

There were many things that the planter had to do for the seed to be in the right place to become a tree that will be productive. The process may be long, and the planter has to constantly water the tree so that it will grow. Manure will also be needed for the tree. If the planter waits patiently, then the seed that has germinated will soon produce a bountiful harvest.

This is similar to those who have big dreams: they must put their dreams to work. Too many people still have their dreams in their storage containers. They must be like the planter and place the seed into the right environment, then constantly provide the tree with water and manure.

Many people are living their dreams today because they took decisive action. They did not wait for others to remove the seed from their storage container, but they removed it themselves and placed it in the right environment. The difference between having dreams and enjoying the results of those dreams is that some dreamers took risks and sowed their seeds with the expectation that their seeds would give them great success.

5.1 Academics

Some persons may have to increase their academics and accelerate their studies. This may be a challenge for them, but they must push past their fears.

Those who have dreams of owning their own business may have to equip themselves with the right knowledge to start and manage their business. Those who have studied many different academic areas may have to make some adjustments to study an additional area that enable them to manage their business successfully.

Some employees know that they are due for a promotion. Therefore, while they wait for their dreams to become reality, they must invest in their academics.

Those who want to study may come up against many obstacles. However, they must make sacrifices if they want to fulfill their dreams.

Figure 1. Studying requires sacrifice

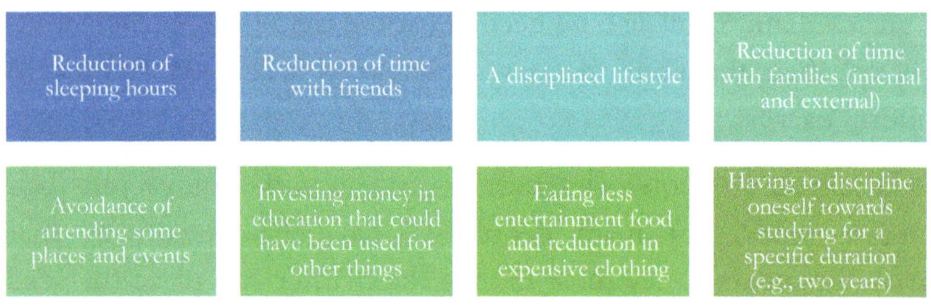

(All figures developed by the author unless otherwise noted.)

When persons study, they have opportunities to increase their values. They are equipping themselves with many opportunities to be promoted or to manage their own business.

The right choice of studies is important for those who want to fulfill their dreams. They may have to spend some time researching the best areas for them to study so that they will fulfill their dreams.

Figure 2. Why is studying essential for you?

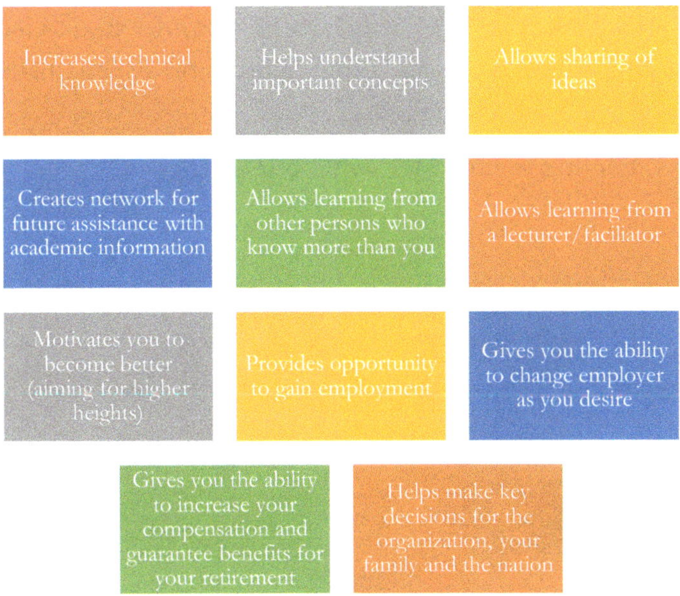

5.2 Skills

Not everyone has to increase their academics to fulfill their dreams. Some people need to increase their skills. This may require them to practice something they are already doing, with the goal of becoming better at that thing. There are other situations where persons will have to learn new skills to fulfill their dreams.

No chef becomes great overnight, but through much trial and error. A carpenter's skills will improve through much practice.

Persons who want to develop their skills may need to associate with others who have similar skills. Many times, learning new skills will take persons out of their comfort zone, but that will be essential for them to become successful.

5.3 Finances

For some dreams to materialize, there must be enough finances to make those dreams come true. The amount of funds needed will vary from person to person, since everyone has their own dream. Not everyone will have the finances they need, so they will have to consider where they will be able to access those funds. If persons do not have all the funds they need, they may have to consider borrowing from financial institutions. Not many people like to borrow, but that may be the only option available to them.

Figure 3. Factors to consider when borrowing

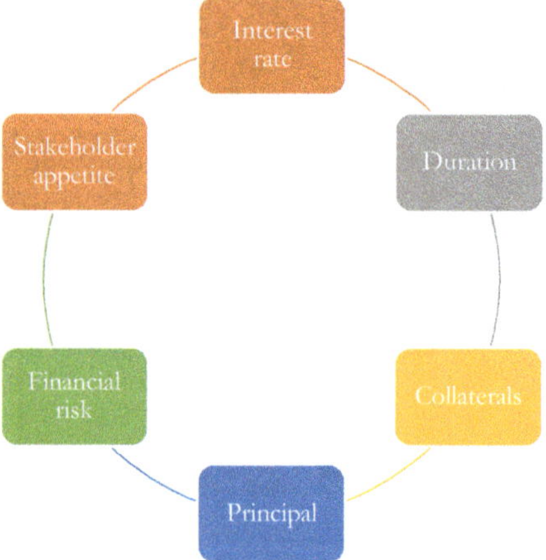

Some people know that their dreams will require them to borrow money. However, there are important factors to consider when deciding to borrow funds. Each of those factors must be carefully analyzed, and if it appears to be too strenuous for the borrower, then other options to finance their dreams must be considered.

The interest rate can be a big turn-off for some people. Most lending institutions have standard requirements for collateral, and not everyone may have the collateral needed.

Figure 4. Collateral required by lending institutions

The borrower must know how much money will be needed to make their dream become a reality. The amount that has to be borrowed will determine the payback period and the duration of the financing.

Borrowers must repay the funds loaned to them. When a good reputation is established, it allows persons to borrow in the future if the need arises.

5.4 Research the resources needed

Each dreamer has work to do. They must assess what they need to do to make their dream a reality and enable them to have a great future. For example, if a person dreams of becoming a great footballer, then they will have to gather information concerning the preparation they need to do and possible clubs to join.

5.5 People

Not all dreams will be fulfilled by the dreamer alone. Sometimes, when one person has a dream, it does not mean that they are the only person who will need to be involved in making the dream a reality.

Researching helps people to know if they need other people to support them. The dreamer may need other persons with similar skills, knowledge, and passion to make their dreams come true. People are key resources in causing dreams to come to life.

Figure 5. Possible persons to make your dreams come true

5.5.1 Family

Sometimes people have not built good relationships with certain family members. However, some persons' dreams may be realized when they communicate and seek help from their family. For example, some family members may be able to provide the finances needed. They may also motivate other family members to fulfill their dreams.

Family members who are living in the same house can constantly motivate each other to go after their dreams. Persons may work longer hours to help a family member to fulfill their dreams. Because of the blood connections in some families, when family members have to do certain activities, they may be able to do so free of cost, since persons do not want to cause a financial burden to allow family members to fulfill their dreams.

5.5.2 Friends

Friends can be a good source of help for some persons to fulfill their dreams. The strong bond shares with certain friends may be so great that they tell their friends about their dreams and personal life.

Some friends are very caring and will help their friends to fulfill their dreams and become successful, even if it means making sacrifices.

5.5.3 Workmates

Those who are employed may keep a close relationship with certain persons at work. Due to their closeness and trust, they will share their dream with selected workmates. Workmates who are genuine will encourage their friends to go after their dreams.

5.5.4 Schoolmates

Persons who were enrolled in learning institutions may stay connected with certain important persons after they have completed their studies. Some schoolmates may be able to share academic information with those who have dreams. Academic persons may also assist with research so that those who have dreams will have easy access to the information they need to know to make their dreams come true.

5.5.5 Neighbors

Most persons have neighbors, and even if they do not see each other daily, they may still maintain good relationships. One neighbor may motivate another to go after their dream. For example, if a person wants to build a large house, they may take inspiration from their neighbors and be motivated to build a large house that is well designed, similar to that of their neighbor.

5.5.6 Religious persons

Some dreams require much prayer. The words shared by religious persons, whether they are ordinary members or the leaders of the congregation, may be just the motivation some persons need to go after their dreams. When religious leaders are not jealous of other persons becoming successful, they will give those who have dreams whatever support they can offer.

6. Writing down dreams

One of the reasons some persons have not fulfilled their dreams is that they have not written down their dreams. When dreams are written down, it allows persons to review them and refresh their minds about what they plan to accomplish or where they plan to go.

6.1 Write down your dreams as early as possible

Oftentimes, people have greater success when they are disciplined. One of the things that disciplined people will do concerning their dreams is to write down what they plan to do. They may not have all the details, but writing down their dreams now will then enable them to determine how they will go after their dreams.

Writing down dreams can be done in detail or summary. However, whatever is written down must be sufficient for the dreamer to know what the dream was and what they plan to accomplish.

For example, if a person's dream is to complete their master's degree, then writing down that dream will remind them that they have something to work towards. They may also have a dream to construct the perfect house. After they write down what they will need to construct the house, then they will have to gather some details about the dimensions of the house.

People must write down their dreams as early as possible. If they allow too much time to elapse, they may forget what they want to accomplish or where they want to go. Everyone must treat their dream as something critical for their future.

6.2 Set timelines

When dreams are written down, it is often important to set timelines. Many dreams will not be accomplished within a few seconds. There may be a series of activities that have to be completed for the dream to be realized.

With timelines, persons know that they have work to do in order to make their dreams a reality. Even if they were undisciplined before they had big dreams, once they have timelines, they will be pressed towards meeting those timelines.

6.3 Identify possible outcomes

With the dream of completing a master's degree or constructing a house, the dreamer needs to assess the possibilities of both dreams becoming a reality shortly. For some persons, it may be easy to complete the master's degree first, since it can be done within two years and the cost for is minimal compared to constructing a house.

Before a person can construct a house, they need to acquire the land, which may be a time-consuming process. If a person needs land in a specific community, then they may have to wait until the government is selling land to people who want to live there, or until someone is selling their land in that community.

Many times, when people have dreams, they are only thinking of one outcome. However, there are often many outcomes to the same dreams, so all possible outcomes must be considered. Some of the possible outcomes will be affected by time, money, and the people involved in the process.

Identifying possible outcomes opens up the dreamer's eyes to see many other ways of accomplishing the same goals. Those who will engage in research may find easier ways of accomplishing their dreams. What many other persons failed to accomplish in times past may become very easy because enough research was done to find alternatives that are easy to execute.

6.4 Eliminate some alternatives

Whenever research is done, it is important to eliminate any alternatives that are too time-consuming or costly. After eliminating some alternatives, the dreamer will have a narrow focus on what has to be done. Therefore, all resources will be aligned with one alternative so that their dream will be accomplished promptly and at a satisfactory cost.

6.5 Alignment of mind and body

When dreams are written down, it causes the mind and body to synchronize. Instead of going in a different direction, the body will conform to what the mind wants to do. There is so much effort that people must put in just to make sure that their dreams will be materialized. When the mind and body are aligned, it causes persons to be disciplined.

6.6 The dream remains fresh

When the dream is written down, it remains fresh in the mind of the dreamer. They can go back to their dream frequently to see what they have written down about it and what they have planned to accomplish.

When a person reads the same information over and over again, it tends to stay with them. Even when they are experiencing discouragement, they can read their dream once again to refresh their mind.

Not everyone likes the idea of writing down their dream, so it may have to be a new culture that they will embrace. This change may enable them to accomplish more things because they are more disciplined now than when they did not have a dream.

When people are very busy or are experiencing difficult situations, they may not remember their dreams. However, when the dreams are written down, it is there for them to see as often as they like, so they can always revisit their dreams.

7. Working hard and smart

Many people have big dreams, but then relax instead of taking action. Dreams will only become reality when decisive actions are taken in a timely and consistent manner. Lack of action will result in the death of dreams.

Many persons could have accomplished many things, but they did not do anything after they had their dreams. Some have listened to people who discourage them, and that has prevented them from going after their dreams.

7.1 Dreams require your input

Many dreams will materialize when the dreamer is willing to make positive input. If the dreamer does not show any interest in their own dream, then who else will be interested in following up with it?

For example, if a person wants to increase their academics, then they have to determine what area of study will be best suited for them. They will have to complete the applications, pay the fees, and then await approval. When they have successfully entered the program, then they will have to listen to the lecturer, ask questions, and study for the examination. On the date of the examination, they must arrive on time and follow the instructions. After the examination is completed, then they have to await the results.

These are some of the many activities that must be executed by someone who wants to increase their academics. Their success will finally come after they complete the examination. The duration of the program may be lengthy, but after they have graduated, they will recognize that people will respect them more and compensate them for their increase in academics.

A similar thing happens for those who have dreams of any kind. They must be willing to give their input so that they will see their dreams manifested before them.

7.2 Work hard

The fulfillment of some dreams requires hard work. The dreamer will have to put in much effort to make their dreams come alive. It may even cause the dreamer to have sleepless nights because it is so important for them to go after their dreams.

For example, many people have large businesses today. However, the businesses they have today came as a result of their very hard work in their younger days. While other people were relaxing, they were constantly working in order to accomplish their dreams.

Those who have completed their examinations had to make great sacrifices to keep studying. They had to study many kinds of literature. Some days they were tired, but they pushed past their tiredness and circumstances, and today they are enjoying their success.

Those who now have houses remember the struggles they went through. Some were turned down by one financial institution, but they were persistent and eventually received the finances to build their house. When the house was under construction, they visited it often and continually encouraged the contractor to complete the house according to the architectural drawing and within the cost allocated for the construction.

Success often demands hard work. The benefits are sweet, but they only come after time and effort are invested to make the dreams come true.

7.3 Determination

A person who will make their dream become a reality must demonstrate determination. While many things will work against them, they must push past the fear and the negative thoughts of others.

An athlete running a marathon will have to keep reminding himself or herself that they have a long distance to go and must remain focused. After the marathon starts, the athlete must manage their energy throughout the journey. They must pace their actions and then ensure that they are ahead of the other competitors when they reach the finish line.

Some athletes may be slow starters, but they know that they have to keep increasing their speed. Shortly after the marathon starts, many athletes will be ahead of them, but during the run, they will begin to overtake the other athletes and eventually get to the head of the race. Their effort to come from behind and finish the marathon in first place will take much determination. No one will accomplish anything significant if they are willing to quit in the face of adversity. There will always be many obstacles for those who have dreams, but as persons remain determined to go forward, they will soon overcome many of those obstacles.

Some persons see obstacles as setbacks, but others see them as building blocks in their quest for success.

7.4 Work smart

Not every dream requires much strength to complete. Some persons have accomplished many things by using wisdom rather than strength. Working smart often requires careful planning and great execution. It also requires the input of other persons who are sufficiently skilled and disciplined in their execution.

Some people are still struggling with their dreams because they are using too much energy and not enough wisdom. They are trying to do everything by themselves. In many cases, leaders do not have to do everything for themselves; they can work through people to get things done.

Employers often allocate certain employees to particular positions because those employees understand what they have to do and will work smart to get their assignments completed promptly. When persons work smart and complete their work in a prompt and accurate manner, they are often rewarded.

Many dreamers must allow their own knowledge and experience to guide them. In cases where they do not know what to do, they must seek guidance from those who are willing to help them.

When persons have dreams, it does not mean that they have to execute those dreams independently. The help of others is often needed to make dreams become reality.

7.5 Do not try to please people

Those who are working hard and smart must do so not to please others but to work towards their own dreams. Too many people focus on working hard to please others. As they do that, they often miss out on fulfilling their dreams and can even make major mistakes.

Those who focus on pleasing others sometimes exert too much energy in doing simple things. Whenever they work hard, they are looking for applause from those around them.

7.6 Put your brain to work

Those who want to work smart must put their brains to work. They cannot sit down and wait for everyone else to make things happen for them. They will have to identify the possible obstacles they will face and think of solutions.

While they are working, they have to review their actions constantly. In cases where they can improve, they must quickly take the relevant actions to show improvement.

7.7 Develop key skills

Some persons will have to develop key skills in order to work smart. At the beginning of their dreams, they may lack some of the necessary skills, but as they plan to execute their dreams, they will see the need to develop those skills in order to achieve success.

A person who has a dream of becoming a chef and owning their own business will have to learn cooking and business management skills. If the person only knew how to prepare a few meals at first, then significant efforts must be made to learn to prepare a greater variety of meals. They may also have to learn how to prepare meals for persons who are affected by different health challenges.

A person who wants to be a great race car driver must learn the rules of the sport and practice driving in dry and wet weather. As they become more skillful in their driving, they can manage various driving conditions.

Dreamers must make a great effort to want to know more. They must make the effort to develop their skills promptly, since they do not have until eternity to accomplish their dreams. Persons who take too long to develop their skills may not be able to fulfill their dreams, since some dreams are time-sensitive.

For example, a person who wants to become a great singer has to develop their singing skills and release their songs in the right season. Once the season passes, no matter how good a singer they are, they may not be able to make the impact that the world is waiting to hear from great singers.

7.8 Connect with key persons

Sometimes, in order to accomplish great things, dreamers need to connect with key persons. They may have to look for persons who have similar skills, are going in the same direction like them, or will help them to accomplish part of their dreams.

The success of one person may be the result of assistance from others. Lone rangers often take too long and may make many mistakes. They may become fearful as they work towards executing their dreams, and their fears may be their stumbling block.

Connecting with key persons who are willing to share their knowledge and experiences will provide dreamers with additional support and wisdom.

7.9 Identify areas of strength

When some people look at their dreams, they see them as mountains. However, while those dreams will require great effort to accomplish, the dreamers must look at their strengths. Everyone has a weakness, but some people spend too much time thinking about their weaknesses instead of focusing on their strengths. With the strengths they have, they will be able to accomplish many things, and if they choose to network with others, then even greater things will be accomplished.

Everyone has strengths, and they must identify those strengths and continue to build on them. They must spend less time complaining about their weaknesses and pay more attention to the things they can do well.

7.10 Identify and ignore nonessential things

Some people have big dreams, but they spend too much time on nonessential things, wasting time and effort doing things that will not allow them to realize their dreams.

Nonessential things rob persons of their time. These things can suck out their energy and make them weary before they even start their mission.

Many persons have looked back at their past and recognized that they could have gone further if they had concentrated on the essential things. They feel unfulfilled because they spent too much time on things that did not add any value, and they wish they could have done better. However, it may be too late for some people, since they have exerted too much time and effort on nonessential things.

Life does not provide people with too many opportunities to do the same thing. For some people, if they miss their time and season, then that is the end of their dreams. For those who are about to begin following their dreams, it is important to learn from the mistakes of others and choose the best things to do now that will allow the dreams to be realized.

7.11 Seek help when necessary

Smart people who want to accomplish their dreams often seek help from others. They know that they do not know everything and are not skilled in every area. They are willing to put aside any pride they may have and ask for help.

They may even seek help from persons who are younger than them, but who have the necessary skills and knowledge. It is better to seek help and be successful with your dream, rather than to remain quiet and be a failure.

8. Learning to be quiet

Dreamers sometimes have to learn to be quiet. Even though they have big dreams, being quiet is important. They must not tell their dreams to everyone, and there are also some things that they will learn when they are quiet.

8.1 Meditate on the dream

When a person has a big dream, they must take some time to meditate on it. They must give themselves time to think about their dream and how it can become a reality.

Many people fail to accomplish their big dreams because they were in too much of a hurry. They are not expected to be slothful concerning their dreams, but they must take the time to meditate on their dreams.

As they meditate, they may receive more inspiration about how to execute their dream. Meditating will allow them to relax their nerves and give them time to think more deeply about their dream.

8.2 Choose who to tell the dreams to

Some people become excited when they have a dream and want to tell everyone about it. However, they must be selective about who they tell their dreams to, which may be a challenge. Not everyone will wish them well, and some people will only say negative things about their dreams. Therefore, selecting certain people to tell about the dream will allow many dreamers to receive constructive feedback, which will motivate them to go after their dreams.

8.3 Avoid telling too many persons

When some persons are experiencing depression, they may shut themselves away. This will only cause them to feel even more depressed, which is a bad practice. However, when people have big dreams, they must avoid certain people. If they tell their dreams to such people, they may receive negative feedback, as not everyone will celebrate the future directions of others.

The more some persons share their dreams with others, the more negative feedback they will receive. Even sharing big dreams with certain family members may not always be the best thing to do, because some family members will identify all the shortcomings rather than the possibilities for success.

8.4 Stop talking about the dream, but spend more time planning

At a certain point, you will need to stop your discussions with many persons concerning your dream and spend more time planning. Devote more time to planning and less time to talking. When more time is spent on planning the dream, more things will be accomplished.

Planning can be time-consuming for those who have big dreams. This means that you must use the available time for planning, not for trying to keep others informed of the dream or to defend why the dream will be accomplished.

For big dreams to be accomplished, it does not require the input of many persons, but just a few persons who have a similar passion for making the dreams come alive. Therefore, select those few supportive persons, tell them about your dreams, and get them to provide you with support. They may also assist with ideas for how to plan for the big dreams to become reality.

It is also important to choose wisely what will be said to certain persons. Not everyone should be given many details.

8.5 Listen to wise counsel

There is great wisdom in listening to wise counsel. Therefore, when you listen to them, be quiet and allow them to do most of the talking. Allow them enough time to share their wisdom. It might be important to write down or record some of the wisdom they share, as wise people may not always have much time to share the same information repeatedly.

8.6 Turn off the telephone

Sometimes, to be quiet, it will be necessary to turn off the telephone. This can help to shut out calls that are not helpful.

When some people know that others have big dreams, they will keep calling them constantly, which can be a distractor. Some of these callers expect to get regular progress reports, and this can be uncomfortable for the dreamer to stop what they are doing in order to explain their progress. With less conversation, more time will be spent on planning or executing the dream.

8.7 Minimize television and newspaper time

Watching the news on television or reading newspapers are two rich sources of information. However, the news that the newspapers and television will present may not be helpful to the dreamer in the current moment. For example, if a dreamer has a plan to make a great impact in the economy with a particular product and the news presents a bad image of the economic condition, it may cause them to give up on their dream.

8.8 Look for a quiet place

Sometimes, persons have to make a desperate effort to find quiet places. This can even mean spending time away from their house. If they go on a vacation, they may choose to go alone, because they want to relax and concentrate on their dreams.

If such persons choose to take a vacation at a resort, they may choose one where there are not too many people, since more people will mean more time for interaction and distraction. Sometimes, people may choose a resort where they are among nature. This allows them to shut out other people and have more time with nature, which may give them more time to concentrate on their dreams.

Those who are employed may choose to visit a resort on the weekend. This will allow them to continue to earn during the week while having time for themselves on the weekend. If there is a great demand to have the vacation during the week, they will have to apply for leave.

Every dreamer must respect themselves and carefully decide how they will use their time. They cannot spend their time trying to meet everyone, since they will be burned out and may become frustrated. Spending some quiet time alone may allow them to see endless possibilities in their dreams. They may appreciate the hard work they will have to do in order to fulfill their dreams.

9. Pray for your dream

Some persons have experienced the power of prayer, so whenever they have a dream, they will pray for their dreams.

Figure 6. Possible reasons to pray for your dreams

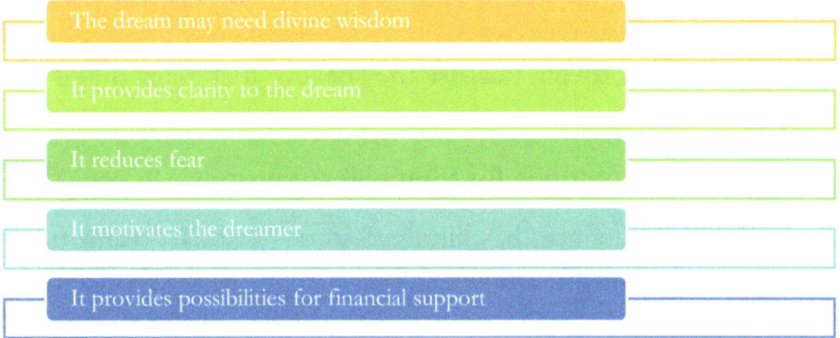

9.1 The dream may need divine wisdom

Some dreams need the wisdom of the Creator. Even highly educated people may not have the answers to their dreams. However, after they pray, they may have the wisdom they need for their dream. With the wisdom and inspiration of the Creator, they will be able to put all the pieces together and receive answers about how to execute their dreams.

9.2 It provides clarity to the dream

Sometimes, dreams need greater clarity, as the dreamer needs to know what to do and when to do it. With prayer, some persons are able to confirm what they have to do and become excited to fulfill their dream.

9.3 It reduces fear

When persons pray, it reduces their fear. They no longer think that their dreams are above their capacity, but they think of themselves as if they will accomplish their dreams.

Once fear goes away, strength will come to those who have prayed. With inward strength, some persons are willing to take on those things that once seemed impossible to them.

9.4 It motivates the dreamer

Dreamers can become more motivated when they pray. They feel comfortable that their prayer will become a reality. They may quickly want to go after their dream because they believe that many things are working in their favor.

9.5 It provides possibilities for financial support

Oftentimes, lack of finances has hindered some persons' dreams from becoming a reality. But after prayer, guidance may be given concerning possible financial support. Doors that once appeared to be closed may soon become open doors that will release finances to the dreamer. The Creator is willing to assist many persons with their dreams. He will also lead people into their lives who have financial resources to assist them with their dreams.

10. Look for similar exposures

Persons with big dreams must look for exposures that are similar to their dreams. While each person's dreams are unique, there are some similarities between them. Therefore, everyone who has a great dream must keep alert and look for similar exposure, through which they may learn many things that will motivate them to fulfill their dream. Some persons just need a boost of confidence in order to take on great dreams.

For example, a young, up-and-coming athlete may look for exposure to participate with accomplished athletes. While the young athlete knows that he or she does not possess the same skills as experienced athletes, it may be an opportunity for growth.

10.1 Grow quickly

Persons with big dreams have to make their dreams become reality very soon. Therefore, they must grow quickly. In areas with much competition, those who take too long to deliver their skills or knowledge may be left behind. In business, organizations that can release their new products to the market more quickly may be able to attract many customers.

For many athletic competitions, people do not remember the names of the athletes who came in second and third. Even if the race ends with a photo finish, people often remember the winner and not those who were right behind them. A similar thing happens for those who have big dreams. If their dreams come through quickly, then people will remember them and respect them.

Every dreamer must be willing to grow quickly. They must challenge themselves to know more and become proficient in whatever they have to do.

10.2 Grow in the right direction

When persons expose themselves to the right experiences, they get to grow in the right direction. They learn from the mistakes of others. They learn about some of the pitfalls and what to avoid. Therefore, most of their energy will be spent doing things that will yield positive results.

Starting in the right direction can ease much tension. Those who start off in the wrong direction may incur many costs and become frustrated in trying to regain their position.

Many people have given up on their dreams because they started off in the wrong direction. After experiencing failure, they lost the zeal to fulfill their dreams. They sometimes live the rest of their lives frustrated that they did not get to fulfill their dreams.

10.3 Learn from others' strengths and weaknesses

There are opportunities to learn from the strengths and weaknesses of others. As persons expose themselves to similar things that others are doing, they will see both the strong and weak areas of those persons.

For example, when a new boxer wants to win their matches and become a great boxer, they will have to watch some videos of their contender. They may also attend some of their contender's boxing matches so that they have great knowledge of their contender's strengths and weakness. Therefore, when they enter the boxing match, they will immediately know how to approach the fight. Within a short time, they can start working on their contender's weaknesses, and if they are successful, they may quickly win the match.

Everyone has weaknesses, which can be identified by those who look carefully. When a person is going after their dreams, they must be open enough for others to tell them of their strengths and weaknesses. Once they are aware of their weaknesses, they will make adjustments so that they will know how to execute their dreams effectively and gain the maximum outcome.

11. Accept failure as a learning moment

Those who are going after a big dream must know that failure will happen. Failure is never a final destination, but an opportunity to utilize other alternatives to get to the same destination at a different time.

11.1 Failure is a part of life

Many times when persons experience failure, they quickly give up, meaning they have given up on their dreams. Those who consistently push hard will recognize that the things that once stood in their path as stumbling blocks were only there to test their tenacity to overcome challenges.

11.2 Failure is not final

Some people freeze when they experience failure. They cry and blame themselves for taking on challenges that look enormous. However, failure is never intended to be final.

If people are going to go after big dreams, they must be aware that big dreams come with big challenges. Those challenges are often many, but they may soon fade away.

11.3 Ride the storms of life

Life is always filled with storms. Those who are not mentally and physically prepared will allow their storms to overtake them. However, great water skiers look for high waves to develop their skills and have fun skiing. What may be dangerous for one person can become fun for others.

Some birds will use strong winds to help them reach their destinations. They will open their wings and soar with the wind. People must take a similar approach when they have big dreams, using their storms to take them to their destinations rather than complaining about challenges.

11.4 Use stumbling blocks as alternative options

Let some stumbling blocks become building blocks that will allow you to accomplish the intended mission. If possible, stand up on the stumbling blocks, as they may provide additional height to climb over walls.

Big dreams are often plagued with many challenges. However, those who want to accomplish their dreams do not spend their days complaining, but they look for suitable alternatives to get to their destination.

When some persons are forced out of a rented home by their landlord, they sometimes make vows to build their own houses. Many of them are now enjoying their houses because their landlords were the stumbling blocks that allowed them to quickly build their own houses. If the landlord had not forced them to move, they might still be paying rent instead of owning their own home.

11.5 Possible solutions when a failure occurs

Not everyone can continue their journey when a failure occurs. However, successful persons have experienced many failures, but they did not allow their failures to stop them from getting to their destinations. A woman who experienced a miscarriage in the first trimester will still try again to become pregnant and give birth to a child. Students who fail their examinations on the first attempt must study the same learning materials and better prepare themselves to take the same examination again.

The success of life does not count how many times a person experiences failure, but their result, which ought to be a success. Strong-willed persons often look for alternatives after failure, but weak-minded people accept failure as their final position.

Figure 7. What to do when failure occurs

11.5.1 Do not blame yourself or others

People can easily become frustrated when a failure occurs. They blame themselves for taking on something too big and may even see themselves as the worst person ever. Sometimes, they blame friends and family members for their failure.

If they continue to blame themselves, they may soon go into a state of depression. They wish that they had not taken on something as important as that big dream. However, they must learn not to blame themselves or others, but to go through their temporary failure until they are victorious.

11.5.2 Do not stress yourself out

Failure can make many persons stress themselves out and have sleepless nights. However, they must learn not to stress themselves out, but to remain calm and look for positive ways to become victorious.

11.5.3 Review possible options

When failure occurs, it may be a good time to review possible options. Some people are narrow-minded and have only looked at one way of accomplishing their dreams, but there are other ways of doing the same things.

Sometimes, the new options will result in less time being taken to accomplish the dreams. New options may also result in less money being spent.

11.5.4 Sing and motivate yourself

Instead of crying when a failure occurs, the same energy can be used to sing. Sometimes, singing may provide the inner strength to take on more challenges. People have to find ways to motivate themselves in the midst of failure. Stress often occurs when there is a failure, but some persons have found great ways to rejoice after failure, since they know that there is little they can do about it in that moment. Stressing about failure may cause them to visit the hospital for stress-related concerns, but rejoicing will make them live longer, happier lives.

11.5.5 Seek advice from competent persons

Many competent persons have good advice to share, especially if they have gone through a similar experience. The advice from competent persons will produce great results with less effort.

Younger persons sometimes learn many things from older persons who have had similar experiences. Parents are often there to advise their children about the right things to do in order to overcome or avoid failure.

11.5.6 Seek much help

Besides seeking advice, it is good to seek help. Some persons have too much pride and do not like to seek help. However, the help they can receive from others will allow them to overcome their failures.

11.5.7 Be patient and joyful

Exercising patience is very important during times of failure. Some storms will not last forever: they will soon vanish as quickly as they came.

In an international heavyweight boxing match, there are twelve rounds. While the opponent may win the first few rounds, the challenger must remain focused and buy some time for the later rounds when the opponent will become tired. When the opponent is tired, there will be a good opportunity for the challenger to be aggressive, and soon the boxing match may be over.

While being patient, try to be joyful. A joyful attitude can produce renewed energy for future successes.

11.5.8 Pray

When all human efforts have failed, then pray. Some persons will choose to pray before they embark on their big dreams, as they execute their dreams, and even when they are finished.

It is important to keep praying as you desire to accomplish your dreams. Prayer provides alternatives that people may not have seen or known of before starting their journey.

12. Work along with a mentor

While many people believe that they can do everything alone, they sometimes realize that they need help. They need someone to mentor them and help them to recognize that they can make their dream come true. Some people have big dreams, but they do not know how and when to start. With the assistance of a mentor in their lives, they will soon take on their dreams and then find the strength to overcome obstacles.

> A mentor is usually someone who has particular relevant experience, knowledge, or skills, and maybe more senior than the person being mentored. The relationship is often specific to a period of transition as someone enters a new role or takes on new responsibilities that are within the mentor's own experience" (Nicholas & Baker, 2013).

Persons who have big dreams may need a mentor to encourage them. The mentor will not be executing the plans for the dreams, but they will be there to share ideas.

The relationship between the mentor and protégé will take some time to develop. Sometimes, when dreamers share their big dreams with selected people, they may find someone who is ready to mentor them. Sometimes, the mentor gives support just because they want to see this individual being successful.

> Most mentoring relationships [are] developed informally as a result of interests or values shared by the mentor and the protégé. Mentoring relationships can also develop as part of a formal mentoring [program]—that is, a planned company effort to bring

together successful senior employees with less-experienced employees. (Noe et al., 2015)

Each mentor may not fill all four of the leading roles that mentors usually provide, but they may fill one or more of these roles (Shields et al., 2016):

Figure 8. Main roles of the mentor

(Developed from Shields et al., 2016)

The mentor may be the broker between the dreamer and other persons who have financial resources. Some mentors may align a protégé with people who have similar dreams so that they will share ideas. The impact of mentors can be great for many dreamers.

For some persons, their mentors have been their role models. Role models are found in many communities. For example, many religious organizations and educational institutions have role models. Some students will discuss certain details with their teachers and lecturers before sharing their dreams with their family members.

Persons who want to get into business may need an adviser. The adviser will ask them important questions and, after much discussion, may share advice with them about how to accomplish their dreams.

When some persons have dreams, they want to accomplish everything in one breath. However, their mentor may advise them on how to break down their dreams into smaller portions and show them which part can start immediately and what will follow later.

A mentor does not always have to be an older person. Some young mentors are willing and able to help persons who are older than them.

Within some families, there may be one person who is the family mentor. Whenever other family members have any concerns, there is at least one family member they can go to for advice.

The work of the mentor is never easy, since a mentor can be overwhelmed with the demand for their time, wisdom, and skills. However, most experienced mentors will manage their time and demand that the protégé complete the assignments.

If a mentor takes on too much, it can cause the protégé to become too dependent. When the protégé becomes too dependent, they will not give much attention to what they have to do, since they are hoping that their mentor will assist them with everything.

The earlier some persons can be weaned off of their mentor, the better it will be for them, as it allows them to grow and develop important skills. Persons must remember that their mentors will not be with them forever, but are only there to assist them with a few assignments.

12.1 Communication with mentors

Those who have mentors in their lives must remember the importance of communication. The absence of communication can cause the protégé to engage in many bad practices at the initial stage.

At the initial stage of the connection between the mentor and protégé, they will have regular communication, perhaps with daily or weekly meetings. However, as the protégé properly manages his or her assignments, the communication between them will become less frequent.

The mentor will often ask many questions at the beginning to get a better understanding of their protégé. The initial conversation may be tense, but as they come to understand each other, their conversation may be like that of two long-standing friends.

Some mentors will share their own experiences with the protégé. As they share their experiences, they will tell the protégé about some of their failures and warn them not to follow those bad examples.

As protégés have victories, they are often excited to share their accomplishments with their mentors. Many mentors are motivated after listening to the accomplishments of their protégés.

12.2 Mentors reduce the time it takes to accomplish dreams

Some persons have not seen the need for a mentor. However, a mentor helps to reduce the time it takes to accomplish certain dreams. Without a mentor, it may take some people a long period of time to accomplish dreams, but when they have mentors in their lives, they can accomplish their dreams within a shorter time.

Most mentors already have shortcuts they can share with their protégés, as they know how to get certain dreams accomplished in the least possible amount of time.

12.3 Mentors reduce possible mistakes

To accomplish some dreams, persons may go through a period of trial and error. However, a mentor will guide the protégé on how to identify and avoid certain mistakes.

If a protégé were to make the wrong mistake, their dreams can be completely destroyed. However, with the assistance of the mentor, such mistakes can be avoided.

When a person shares what their dreams are and how they plan to accomplish them, they will receive guidance from their mentor. Their mentor will share with them some of the things that are not possible and some of the things that will lead to mistakes. Each person's dream is too great for them to risk making mistakes that will prevent them from accomplishing their dreams.

12.4 Mentors provide encouragement

Mentors can provide encouragement to their protégés. There are times when protégés may feel discouraged. However, with the advice of their mentors, they are willing to see past their challenges and utilize their energy to accomplish their dreams.

When the protégé keeps the mentor informed of their progress, the mentor will often provide correction or encouragement. As the protégé improves, the mentor will have more reasons to celebrate the protégé's accomplishments.

12.5 Mentors are often confidential

People often trust mentors to share their dreams and life stories with, because many mentors are confidential and will keep certain private information to themselves.

Since many protégés know that their mentors are confidential, they are willing to share such information with their mentors. Most mentors will give listening ears to their protégés and then offer advice.

Protégés may share more confidential information with their mentors than with their own families. Most mentors know that they have to live up to the expectations of their protégés, so they do not disclose confidential information.

At the beginning of the relationship between the mentor and the protégé, they may not share too many personal details. However, as the relationship grows, they may be more open to each other, so they will talk about more details and personal matters.

13. Allocation timelines for activities

Many people have failed to achieve their dreams because they were poor managers of the time available to them to accomplish their dreams. They are aware that they have big dreams, but they treat their big dreams as ordinary things.

13.1 A bigger dream requires more time for planning

With bigger dreams, there may be the need to spend more time planning. Persons sometimes fail to accomplish big dreams because they treat them the same way as small dreams. Consider the construction of a flat small house for two family members, compared to a two-story house for an extended family. The design and costs will be different for each house.

Figure 9. Why allocate more time for bigger dreams?

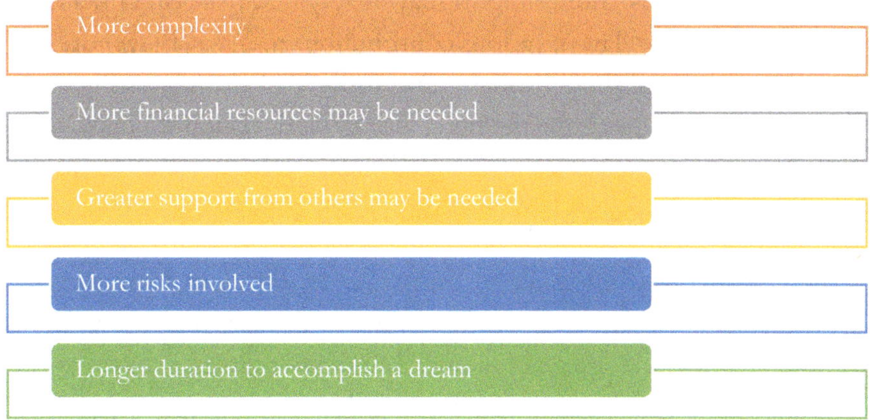

13.1.1 More complexity

Bigger dreams are often more complex. Because of their greater complexity, more time will be required for planning. Attention has to be paid to all of the details and the additional areas.

For example, manufacturing a bicycle is different from manufacturing a motorcycle. While they both have two wheels, the bicycle does not have an engine, while the motorcycle does.

13.1.2 More financial resources may be needed

Oftentimes, bigger dreams need more finances to execute them. The example of building a one-flat house for two family members compared to a two-story house for an extended family demonstrates the need for more money to be budgeted and spent for the construction of the larger house.

Sometimes, seeking external finances will have to be considered. The lending agency will require many documents and will have to ensure that all the legal requirements are met before approving the mortgage. The security deposit needed by a financial institution for small mortgages will be different than what is needed for large mortgages.

13.1.3 Greater support from others may be needed

For bigger dreams, more support may be required from other persons. Each individual will have various contributions to make. Bigger dreams are often accomplished through the assistance of many persons, since one person does not have the time, money, and wisdom to make their big dream a reality alone.

13.1.4 More risks involved

The risk involved in smaller dreams may be different from the risk involved in larger dreams. Sometimes, smaller dreams will be completed by the dreamer alone, but bigger dreams have to be completed over a longer period and with the assistance of more people.

Different dreamers have different risk appetites. Those who are risk-seekers may engage in more activities, which will result in more complexity. A risk-averse dreamer will also have their own set of risks to deal with.

Table 1. Risk preference

Risk Preference	Explanation
Risk averse	A decision maker who acts on the assumption that the worst outcome might occur
Risk neutral	A decision maker who is concerned with what will be the most likely outcome
Risk seeker	A decision maker who is interested in the best outcome no matter how small the chance that they may occur

(Extracted from ACCA P5, 2010)

13.1.5 Longer duration to accomplish a dream

Some small dreams may be completed within a few days or weeks. However, bigger dreams are often completed over a longer duration, perhaps months or years.

The example of the construction of a one-flat house compared to a two-story house illustrates that the time to construct both houses will vary. Because the demands are greater, more time will be needed to complete bigger dreams.

14. Plan and execute your dream

Big dreams require careful planning. Small dreams may be planned by one person, but big dreams may need the work of several persons to plan.

For example, if a person wants to become the president of a university student association, this dream will need the input of others. Specifically, it requires the input of other students who will have to vote for the candidate.

14.1 Plan diligently

Diligent planning will be needed for big dreams. This may require several weeks or months of work, as well as the wisdom of others.

Diligent planning may also require many details. Different scenarios will have to be considered, along with the pros and cons of each one.

As people plan diligently, they will have to be disciplined in writing down their dreams and plans. When they write down their plans, they will have some written information to consult in the event they make a mistake.

Those who engage in diligent planning will need accurate information. For example, persons who want to borrow money to construct a house will need to know the actual interest rates that the financial institutions offer for mortgages.

14.2 Identify possible risks

There will be many risks associated with big dreams. However, if some of those risks are taken into consideration in the initial stage, then at the time of execution, measures will be in place to mitigate the risks that were identified.

> Risk is a condition in which there exists a quantifiable dispersion in the possible results of any activity. (ACCA P1 2009)

Once risks are identified, then the planners need to determine their response to those risks. They may not be able to find solutions for all risks. However, they must have plans to mitigate certain risks if they want to become successful in executing their dreams.

Figure 10. Possible actions that can be taken for risks

(Extracted from ACCA P1, 2009)

The figure above shows four possible actions that can be taken to help persons to achieve their dreams. If dreamers do not want any risk, then they should not consider executing their dreams. Some risks can be avoided and some can be reduced. There are times when people have to accept certain risks, since there is nothing they can do to avoid them. Efforts must also be taken to reduce some risks by looking at possible alternatives.

14.3 Identify opportunities

With careful planning, opportunities must be identified. One big dream can produce many opportunities. There may also be opportunities within the community.

Persons who are working may find opportunities at their places of employment. They might be able to earn more money or save some of their earnings. Persons who have products to sell may be able to sell their products to some of their workmates.

If certain opportunities are not available locally, then overseas opportunities must be considered. There will be risks involved, but the rewards may be greater than the risks, so it may be worthwhile to pursue overseas opportunities.

14.4 Identify partners and engage in networking

Those who were careful to plan how they will execute their dream will have some time to identify the assistance they will need from others. They can partner with persons who are like-minded and want to assist them with their dreams.

If a person's dream is to establish a business, then they may need to network with suppliers and customers, as well as with other businesses in the same industry. Networking has many benefits, two of which are the sharing of ideas and experiences. When experiences are shared, it helps those who are newly entering the business to make progress quickly and avoid certain pitfalls.

14.5 Make the dreams a reality

After much planning, it is finally time to execute the plan. Persons must be prepared to give all of their effort towards their dreams. They are aware that there will be challenges in fulfilling their dreams, but they must remember that they are the only person who has to work towards their dream. While they are working through other people and things to make their dreams a reality, ultimately, they are responsible for making their own dreams come alive, so they must go towards the planned destination. At the initial stage, they may have some resistance, but they must keep pushing until they reach the destination.

Figure 11. Go towards the planned destination

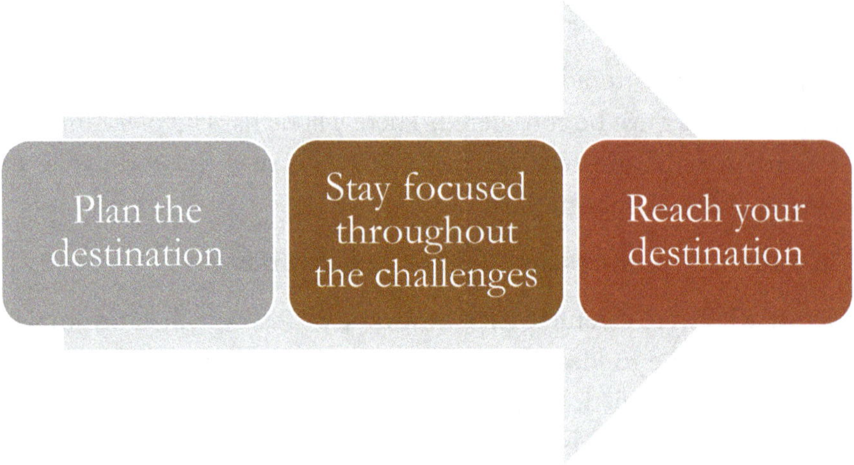

Plan the destination → Stay focused throughout the challenges → Reach your destination

Someone must be the driving force behind all the activities that have been planned. They will have to motivate themselves and must be prepared to climb over some stumbling blocks. There will be risks, but they must remember that their rewards can be greater than their risks.

A runner who has prepared for a race must be willing to participate in it. After they receive the instructions, they will have to go to the starting line. After the sound of the gun, they must run as fast as possible until they pass the finish line. To be declared the winner, they must keep their mind on the finish line and end the race ahead of all other participants.

Those who have dreams must go after their dreams. They must execute their dreams skillfully and promptly. Finally, they must be happy that they have discharged their responsibilities and that their dreams have been realized.

15. Review past performance

After your dreams are executed, it is important to review past performance. This will become important in the future, as it can guide the actions you take for similar dreams. A person who is willing to learn from their past performance can make great progress if they have the opportunity to do something similar in the future.

15.1 Review past performance against plans

It is important to review past performance against the plans that were set. Those who did not plan how to execute their big dreams, will not have anything to measure their performance.

When plans have been written down, this will help with the performance review. The reviewer will be able to measure what was planned and what was executed. The plans that were effectively executed and have yielded the intended results will make the dreamer feel satisfied. When there are areas of failure, it will cause the dreamer to reconsider what they failed to deliver as they had planned.

15.2 Accept past mistakes

When reviewing past performance, persons must be willing to accept their mistakes. They may be surprised by some of the mistakes they made. However, they must remember that all humans will make mistakes.

Some of the mistakes might have been a result of poor planning. Others can be a result of not having the required resources. For example, a lack of funds and support people can lead to mistakes.

Being too anxious to fulfill the dreams can also lead to mistakes. Sometimes, when persons have dreams, they do not want to give themselves enough time to carefully assess the entire situation before going into action.

15.3 Identify areas for improvement

There is often the need to improve on past performance if the same things occur again. Many lessons have been learned about what happened, which may be good information for future successes.

Leaders in organizations will often review the previous year's performance in order to learn about what they need to do for the next financial year. When leaders are preparing annual budgets, they identify the organization's successes and failures in the past year. They often try to build on last year's successes while avoiding last year's mistakes.

16. Celebrate every success

Every success must be celebrated, whether big or small. As people appreciate their successes, they may be motivated to do more things and possibly to take on bigger dreams.

16.1 Acknowledge the commitment and effort

It is important to acknowledge the commitment made in pursuing a dream. There are great efforts that go into making dreams become reality. When persons celebrate their success, they are stirred to do other great things. They see yesterday's victory as a starting point for tomorrow's big dream.

16.2 Acknowledge the contributions of others

It is important to acknowledge the contributions of others who have assisted with the success of a dream. These individuals have made sacrifices because they wanted a friend or family member to become successful.

16.3 Motivate others

When persons celebrate their success, they serve as a reference point for others. When other persons see them overcoming their stumbling blocks and achieving victory, it stirs their passion to work hard and be smart towards their dreams.

Many persons are looking for examples of successful persons, so they will often ask questions of those who have already found success. After they learn what others did to become successful, they will try many of the same things.

Whenever one person accomplishes something, it challenges others to take similar actions. Sometimes, all it takes is for one person to become successful, and very soon, many others are trying the same thing.

For example, if one person starts a business and makes a profit, many others may try the same thing. Very soon, many others will open similar businesses because they want to gain victory.

While progress often breeds enemies, success has a way of attracting more persons to work towards their success. Some persons become restless until they have their victory.

Reference list

ACCA P1. (2009). *Professional accountant.* BPP House.

ACCA P5. (2010). *Advanced performance management.* BPP House.

Nicholson, F., & Baker, C. (2013). *Certification in risk management assurance.* Institute of Internal Auditors Research Foundation (IIARF).

Noe, R. A., Hollenbeck, J. R., Gerhart, B., & Wright, P. M. (2015). *Human resource management: Gaining a competitive advantage* (9th ed.). McGraw-Hill Education.

Shields, J., Brown, M., Kaine, S., Dolle-Samuel, C., North-Samardzic, A., McLean, P., Johns, R., O'Leary, P., Plimmer, G., & Robinson, J., (2016). *Managing employee performance and reward: Concepts, practices, strategies* (2nd ed.). Cambridge University Press.

About the author

Having big dreams was never in the mind of Geary Reid. However, as he worked, studied, served the Creator, and interacted with people, he recognized that he has an appetite for big dreams. He is not afraid to take on big challenges, because he has learned to network with others.

Geary Reid has learned not to tell everyone about his big dreams. He often stays quiet and plans how to execute his dreams. He tries to expose himself to many different conditions and people so that his appetite for greatness will always be there. Over the years, he has experienced many failures, but he often looks for alternatives. He often challenges himself to do great things. Many times, he has used failure as a learning moment, so his confidence grows whenever he fails.

Working hard and being smart are some of the things he has learned that are necessary for those who have big dreams. Therefore, he is often mentally prepared to work hard. When others are resting, he tries to take a little time and make great things happen. With his academic accomplishments, he writes down his big dreams, then plans how to execute them. When planning the execution of his dreams, he takes into consideration the finances that will be needed and the possible risks that are associated with each dream.

Reid has also spent much time encouraging people to go after their big dreams. There are times when he will assist persons with planning the execution of their big dreams. He likes motivating people to give their best effort and reminding them not to spend time listening to toxic people.

Some persons have acted as mentors in Reid's life, and he is thankful for all his mentors, which include persons like his parents, teachers, neighbors, workmates, and religious persons. Each of these persons has helped his confidence to grow. They have also helped to encourage him and show him ways to become successful. Geary Reid remains thankful for all the support he has received from others. He is willing to take advice and constructive criticism from anyone, no matter their age.

The accomplishment of big dreams requires the input of many persons. Therefore, Geary Reid has a network that includes many people. He shares his ideas with certain people and listens to their feedback. While some people run away from their big dreams, Geary Reid constantly looks for opportunities to experience more big dreams. He knows that every big dream will create a positive impact in the lives of many people.

www.ingramcontent.com/pod-product-compliance
Lightning Source LLC
LaVergne TN
LVHW010358160826
845677LV00005BA/1308

* 9 7 8 9 7 6 8 3 0 5 8 6 2 *